CountryLiving

storage style

CountryLiving

storage style

PRETTY AND PRACTICAL
WAYS TO ORGANIZE
YOUR HOME

Lesley Porcelli

HEARST BOOKS
New York

PAGE 1: A vintage filing cabinet is all business as a sideboard in a dining room. Generously sized drawers provide lots of space for table linens, silverware, candle?sticks, and other tableware; its surface is roomy enough to hold serving platters and become part of the buffet. The nearly square Victorian botanical prints hung above complement the cabinet's boxy drawers, the color combination standing out beautifully in the white room.

PAGE 2: Magazines have a way of accumulating in any room of the house, but especially in the living room. Here, a space too awkward for a bookshelf is fitted with a slim rack for magazines, making it easy to keep them from gathering under the sofa or on the coffee table.

PAGE 6: A plate rack has been installed between two window frames, an ingenious use of space that also allows the home's original brick walls to show through. The white platters and plates gleam against the textured background provided by the bricks. A pot rack hangs from the original tin ceiling, supporting antique copper pots and pans as well as garlic. The work island's sides match the Shaker-style wainscoting original to the house.

Library of Congress Cataloging-in-Publication Data

Porcelli, Lesley.
 Country Living storage style : pretty and practical ways to organize your home / Lesley Porcelli.
   p. cm.
 Includes index.
 ISBN-13:978-1-58816-660-9
 ISBN-10: 978-1-58816-660-0
 1. Storage in the home. I. Title.
 TX309.P66 2008
 648'.8—dc22

2007019596

10 9 8 7 6 5 4 3 2 1

HEARST BOOKS
New York

An Imprint of Sterling Publishing
387 Park Avenue South
New York, NY 10016

First Paperback Edition 2012.

Country Living is a registered trademark of Hearst Communications, Inc.

www.countryliving.com

For information about custom editions, special sales, premium and corporate purchases, please contact Sterling Special Sales Department at 800-805-5489 or specialsales@sterlingpub.com.

Distributed in Canada by Sterling Publishing
C/o Canadian Manda Group, 165 Dufferin Street Toronto, Ontario, Canada M6K 3H6

Distributed in Australia by Capricorn Link (Australia) Pty. Ltd., P.O. Box 704, Windsor, NSW 2756 Australia

Manufactured in China

ISBN: 978-1-58816-994-5 (paperback)

contents

foreword

if there's one thing we could all use more of, it's storage
space. And if you're a collector, it can be especially challenging to find room for all your treasures. Filling oversized storage bins with collectibles, kitchenware, or winter clothes is one way to keep closets and cupboards under control, but it's certainly not the most aesthetically pleasing way. Wouldn't it be lovelier to keep the things you love close at hand, artfully tucked away in an armoire, antique trunk, or vintage suitcase?

Country Living Storage Style is here to help. On the pages ahead you'll find dozens of storage solutions that are not only practical but pretty. There are ideas for every room in the house, from elegant living rooms and serene bedrooms to efficient home offices and humble mudrooms. Easy-to-follow advice on such topics as hiring a professional organizer and storing fine tableware will help you rid your home of clutter and care for what you have. The "Reinvent It" boxes scattered throughout the book show how to transform flea market finds into useful storage. Now a day spent antiquing can actually give you more space to store and display your prized possessions. That's advice we all can follow!

The Editors

introduction

whether home is a nineteenth-century farmhouse rooted on a hill, a two-story saltbox on a tree-lined street, or a tiny cottage at the end of a winding road, stepping in the front door after time away is to meet relief for the spirit, an escape into the privacy and comfort that sometimes we forget we need. Home is the place where we keep all our treasured possessions, but also the quotidian ones; it is the place where we feed and bathe ourselves and kiss our families goodnight. The little details of home assume meanings that the casual visitor could never know, and, ideally, they wrap us in a security blanket of contentment, endearing themselves to us as we go about our lives, every object a reminder of and a reconnection with our individuality. The gleam of the antique stove as you put the kettle on for tea; the feel of the living room carpet underfoot when you curl up on the sofa with a newspaper; crawling under your grandmother's quilt in winter, and—your storage.

In an empty foyer, just one pair of kicked-off boots and one wet umbrella would constitute disarray, but here, providing designated spaces for such items not only helps arrange them neatly, but contributes an easy sense of style to the whole space. A cushion-topped bench of cubbies holds shoes and baskets of sweaters, shawls, scarves, and hats; a metal tray catches drips from rain boots and umbrellas; and a coat rack extends branches for jackets and wraps. A fabric bulletin board with pockets holds mail and extra sets of keys.

If you're like most people, that word fell like a stone, and with good reason. The cold practicality of such a concept seems to undermine the very notion of seeking comfort at home, where emotion, not practicality, rules the roost. There's nothing enticing in thinking about storage space, and since most of us feel that we have too little of it, the thought alone can overwhelm to the point where we postpone dealing with it for as long as possible. And this would be fine, except that little by little, a lack of attention to clutter eats into the edges of home's serenity—the stacks of DVDs surrounding the television, shoes and winter coats spilling from the closets, and the kitchen cabinets a jumble of things we don't use or even remember.

The solution is rarely found in the new generation of home-organization stores, which intimidate all but the most enthusiastic of organizers with their strictly utilitarian bins and boxes fashioned from wire and molded plastic— frankly, if you enjoyed the process of shopping there, you would most likely not be seeking ideas in a book like this one. Nor does a book with the efficiency of Mary Poppins, prodding you to set up schedules and charts for purging the entire house, encourage the reluctant.

That's not the approach we're interested in here. All the promise of a well-organized life will only jump-start so many people. The result is too vague, and the upkeep too unimaginable to inspire sacrificing even a single precious evening or weekend to the cause.

Instead, we suggest coming to organization through a back door, that is, viewing storage solutions in a way that makes them pleasurable, not tedious. For decades the dream homes—but more important, the real homes—that have appeared in *Country Living* have inspired readers with their comfortable mix of great looks and inviting, lived-in approachability, and when we looked more closely at many of these homes, we noticed clues to their welcoming style hiding in plain sight. In some cases, the storage tricks and organizing arrangements were the very things that set the tone for a whole room, that infused the space with the personalities of the people who lived there. What you or I might put off for its sheer drudgery—say, organizing the spice rack or creating order among a china collection—these homeowners had attacked with a wit and flair that ultimately made each home unique, stylish, and unforgettable.

And so, here is what we propose: Rather than look at this book with that New-Year's-resolution sort of good intention mixed with secret dread, resolve to read it at leisure. Make yourself some tea or hot chocolate, put your feet up, and let yourself delight in these pages. We suspect the most wonderful thing will happen: You'll begin to see organization in a whole new way—not as a separate entity from the design and decoration of your home, but as an integral element of its style. And certainly, before you close the book, you'll see some ideas that excite you enough to move you into action. In our view, this is the simplest and most enjoyable way to approach storage, but also the most logical. After all, the best ideas for organizing will never work if implementing them or using them is inconvenient, uncomfortable, or annoying, and if they don't enhance your home.

And the same goes for the rest of your family. Of course, children resist putting things away when the task is so seemingly insurmountable—all their toys scattered across the den have to make it all the way up the stairs and down the hall to their bedrooms? An ottoman that doubles as a storage chest for their favorites will be a benefit for all—they'll love hiding their things away in this secret spot (and be more easily convinced that the spillover has got to be put elsewhere) and you'll wonder how you ever lived without this easy solution. Thus, you see how the Shaker adage "a place for everything and everything in its place" requires not superhuman discipline, but a little bit of clever planning.

In addition to this new view of storage as attractive and suitable to your life and style, we do suggest holding one concept in your mind as you read this book: Note how storage is either concealed, as in trunks, cabinets, and closets, or on display, as in shelving, counters and tabletops, wall hangings, and so forth. Why the distinction? If your clutter is the type that's not particularly aesthetic—such as DVDs, bath and

cleaning products bought in bulk, and out-of-season clothing—you'll want to pay particular attention to your strategies for concealment. On the other hand, if you have an overabundance of attractive things—an expansive collection of pitchers, too many precious photos to stash away in a box somewhere, more books than you'd like to admit—then storage that crosses over into the display category will often prove a satisfying solution. In these pages you'll see a mix of both open and hidden storage, as well as ideas for mixing storage and display. These ideas transcend style, so they'll work whether your taste is for country chic, rustic, retro, or even urban flea market. Since the best storage doesn't look like storage, you'll notice how antique shop bargains and household castoffs can find a whole new useful life solving your organizing problems. Moreover, you'll learn to examine all the space in your home—even that which you've taken for granted in the past—and how to play with it, how roominess affords the opportunity for display, and how furniture that does double duty, like a small dresser that becomes a nightstand or a coffee table with drawers in it, will elegantly come to the rescue.

Included are lots of practical pointers, smart tips, and inspiring solutions to help you organize as much or as little as you wish. We hope you'll refer to this book again and again through the years; fresh eyes will find something new every time you look through it. Enjoy.

CHAPTER ONE living and dining rooms

perhaps because they are the most public rooms—the first faces of your home that a guest might see—we sometimes forget that living and dining rooms are also where everyone in the home spends time together every day. The desire to keep these rooms neat and to enjoy living in them can seem contradictory, but the intersection of these ideals can actually provide a starting point for infusing every corner with style and functionality.

Left unchecked, clutter will naturally build, the evidence of daily life, but banishing it completely is a losing battle. The key is to keep it under control with storage that is effortless, and just as important, seamlessly integrated into the look of the room. This means, for example, an antique toy chest that kids will love rifling through to find their board games (and thus, will be less resistant to putting them away) which can double as a coffee table. In another home, a few baskets

Two matching Shaker-style cabinets constructed from recycled wood echo the lines of the fireplace and have the classic look of built-ins. Their sheer depth and opaque doors enclose a large amount of storage space, all while maintaining the spare, easy elegance of the room. As their tops visually extend the mantel, they provide additional surface area to display decorative objects, with enough spacing in between them to maintain that clean aesthetic.

tucked under a side table to catch magazines, books, and knitting will be perfect for the job. Perhaps an armoire large enough to contain a television and CD player, along with the accompanying movies and music, will answer the call to order in your house, or maybe simply a second sideboard will provide your burgeoning china collection with both display and storage space. Whatever the case, these rooms are about coming together with family and friends and unwinding, and you'll know that you have hit upon the right combination of style and comfort when you find yourself doing so more often.

Open storage satisfies our desire to create order and at the same time surround ourselves with things we love. This room's existing architecture offers unexpected opportunities for storage and display. Between the exposed wall studs of this informal beach house hang shelves at varied heights, perfect for books, board games, photos, and seashells, which become the central character and focal point of the space. A pine trunk topped with a cushion is roomy storage masquerading as a window seat. A basket is also put to work storing additional books. Despite the stripped-down décor, a few fanciful touches give the room an understated elegance: prints and art mixed with the books, a gilt mirror over the sofa, and porcelain vases for dramatic flower arrangements.

OPPOSITE: Train your eye to look for storage potential in unexpected places. Here, the backs of two church pews were transformed into display cases and affixed to the wall. Painted white outside and black inside, they hold a set of ironstone platters safely in place and act as display cases for the collection. The black interiors highlight the graceful shapes of the platters.

RIGHT: Here's an example of how adding a new piece of furniture can have the effect of making a room feel bigger: This corner cupboard fits into a space that would otherwise go unutilized. Corner cupboards work magic for both display and storage, and the combination—upper shelves and counter for a few treasured collectibles and hidden storage below—is ideal for a living or dining room.

ABOVE LEFT: A shot of breezy style comes from an unlikely source: chicken wire fronting a flea-market hutch. But beside the novelty of the wire itself, the openness of the piece converts the cabinet into a visual extension of the room, where a collection of gorgeous blue McCoy vases invites the eye to peek inside. Books and blankets in view and within easy reach further enhance the comfortable spirit behind such a setup.

BELOW LEFT: Silverware sorted in antique trophies makes a winning combination; the splendid patina on the latter underlines the gleam of the former, and setting the table has never been such a carefree affair. Though the dainty sugar bowl is crystal rather than metal, its double ears make it a great team player.

OPPOSITE: Even disparate collections can come together with amazing effect. Here, vintage clocks, trophies, and dog figures are grouped in this old-fashioned medical cabinet, keeping them safe from prying fingers but still on display.

ABOVE & RIGHT: Here's a living room in which lots of comfortable living takes place: Barn-style shutters front the floor-to-ceiling cupboards on either side of the fireplace, punctuating the rustic, but very chic room; painted white, they blend with the walls, masking their generous size. By hiding the TV and other items, they preserve the fireplace as the room's focal point. Combined with the trunk-turned-coffee table, the storage possibilities are limitless: Movie and music collections, books, photo albums, and games all have plenty of room.

LEFT: A modern space-saver that was unavailable to most just a decade ago—a plasma-screen television hung over the mantel like a piece of artwork—makes room for additional luxuries; in this case, custom-built bookshelves and a full bar with a wine cooler, both of which provide this small room with ample storage

keeping clutter at bay

it's a fact of life that the more traffic that passes through a space, the more accumulation naturally builds. In order to battle clutter in any room of the house, it helps to think about the reasons why—and there are several.

Clutter is caused by postponing decisions. If you can't decide what action to take with a piece of mail, for example, it is often added to a "to do" stack that can sit for weeks. When something new enters the house, select a home for it right away, and put it there diligently.

If you have a hard time putting something away in its designated home, say, the food processor in an upper cabinet, it is probably because it is not a particularly well-suited spot for it. If you use your food processor several times a week, it may be too tedious to get out the stepladder and put it away on a high shelf so often. This is a candidate for a more accessible cabinet or for leaving out on the countertop permanently.

You may have one system working when you actually need two. Divide storage systems into "present" and "long-term" or "out-of-season." In the case of a coat rack or exposed hooks, only coats, hats, and bags that are worn in the current season should be kept there; the rest should be hung in a closet or put into trunks until the appropriate season. The same goes for all rooms of the house: In winter, rotate your ice-cream maker and grilling equipment into a high cabinet and keep your stew pots and roasters close by.

If kids' toys are always underfoot in a particular room of the house, such as the family room, consider giving them a little space of their own. Assign a series of cubbies, a toy chest, or one of the lower shelves on the bookshelves for them to keep their things; it will make tidying up a lot easier for them *and* you.

Your mother always said it, and it was true: If you devote a few minutes each day to picking up, it will prevent little jobs from snowballing into big ones. Set aside a few minutes at the end of each session at your desk or in the kitchen to neaten up and get ready for the next time.

Though this room appears casual, a strict color scheme allows its ample shelving to become a defining element of its great style. Open in the back to showcase the orange walls, the white shelves feature an excellent example of combining hardworking storage with display space for personal treasures. Photos, books, and accessories are artfully arranged with storage boxes and baskets. A weathered white folding table also fits right in, its surface generous enough to accommodate more display.

OPPOSITE: A hand-painted antique trunk is so handsome as a side table that you barely notice the roomy storage hidden in plain view. Blankets, board games, and family photo albums can be stored here yet easily accessed. Firewood is stored in a sturdy basket.

CLASSIC COUNTRY

Baskets have an inherent warmth and have long been a staple of country-style storage. They can stand alone or be tucked under tables and beds, or even mixed among books and other items on shelves.

RIGHT: Don't write off baskets as suitable only for the more casual rooms of your house. The clean lines of these woven boxes make them sophisticated enough for this formal interior, as they virtually become part of the furnishings: Here, they serve as filing cabinets, converting otherwise unused space into attractive storage.

5 great ideas from this room

1 Custom-built egg-crate shelving mimics the ceiling's exposed white beams.

2 The multiple shelves provide ample room to mix storage and display. Framed prints, vases, and mementos are mixed with magazine files, baskets, and boxes.

3 White magazine organizers crisply echo the white shelves.

4 An alcove large enough to fit a desk was incorporated into the shelves' design.

5 Small containers—a mix of magazine organizers, baskets, boxes, and creamers—provide storage for periodicals, stationery, and painting and office supplies and creates a pleasing, layered mix of objects.

OPPOSITE: Though similar in theory to a bookshelf, this unit of cubbies invites a more playful mix of books and display objects. Vintage toys and a casual arrangement of Americana reflect the primary color scheme of the living room, allowing the more subtle colors of the book spines to blend in demurely.

OPPOSITE: A well-worn bench painted ebony provides high contrast in this white, sun-drenched room, and it serves as an improvised bookshelf that doesn't obstruct the windows. In addition to providing a home for treasured books, the scale and colors of the setup visually anchor one side of the sunroom.

Reinvent It

A stepped plant shelf can be given a fresh coat of paint and transformed into a bookshelf. Binoculars and their leather case, both attractive enough to display, mix with the volumes to add a lovely texture to the arrangement, as does the topping of fresh hydrangeas in a silver cup.

A gorgeous mix of storage and display: The enormous antique library display cases, bought at auction for $200, are quite at home here, complementing the extra-long dining table (fashioned from an old barn door, mounted on porch posts, and topped with glass) and the spacious dining room. The oversized scale of the cases provides a dramatic backdrop for an extensive collection of creamy white and floral china; the doors on the lower portion are lined with curtains, so that more utilitarian pieces can be stored out of sight.

31

OPPOSITE: An avid collector with a limited amount of space, this home-owner turned to two classics for storage solutions: The white armoire hides the television set and showcases a collection of McCoy and Shawnee pottery, while a stack of vintage suitcases stores table linens and sheets. Contributing to the sense of order despite the large number of objects is the way each grouping is positioned by size, creating little pockets of symmetry in the deliberately asymmetrical arrangement of the space.

RIGHT: Go ahead, crowd your display cabinet—when everything in it and even the room itself are of the same hue, large groupings can never seem in disarray. In shades of white, this collection of 1930s and '40s McCoy pottery, as well as compatible pieces found during the past ten years, is a serene work of art. Glass doors keep the collection safe from dust and breakage.

OPPOSITE: A collection of pressed leaves, framed and hung in a grid, mimics the grid of the old general-store drawer unit. The drawers are an ideal organizer for pens, pencils, stationery, or hobby supplies, and the piece is placed atop a bench to achieve a comfortable height. There's also space underneath the bench for storage—in this case, a basket. Books stacked on top act as pedestals for a collection of green-glazed Ohio pottery.

LOOK ABOVE AND BELOW The space above an armoire or under a bench or side table is often the perfect spot to tuck a basket or suitcase, adding instant storage to otherwise unused space.

ABOVE: Painted boxes and blanket chests number among early America's most elaborately decorated pieces of furniture, perhaps because they were meant to safeguard personal treasures. These chests provide capacious storage and are often family heirlooms, handed down from one generation to the next.

RIGHT: Vintage suitcases hold this homeowner's old report cards, photos, and other paper memorabilia. Each case is affixed with a hangtag labeled with the contents, making items easy to find. By placing the suitcases on the lower shelf of the cart, normally over-looked space is put to good use. Suit-cases make terrific long-term storage.

working with professional organizers

think of the most cluttered room of your house. Now imagine a stranger coming in and giving that room a complete makeover, helping you get rid of things you no longer need and finding logical homes for the things you do. It may sound like a fantasy, but this is exactly what a professional organizer does. But lest the thought of all that organizing sound cold and impersonal or inspire a vision of unattractive plastic containers, take heart. Most professional organizers agree that the idea that everyone who works with them will have to buy lots of plastic tubs or accept a new, superhuman discipline to stay neat is completely false. Rather, organizers come up with a system that's right for you and your style, and the system should keep working long after the organizer is gone.

The best way to find a professional organizer is through word of mouth; you can also search for one by entering your zip code at the website of the National Association of Professional Organizers, napo.net. Don't straighten up or do anything at all to prepare for the professional organizer's visit—they need to see exactly how you've been living and working. But do keep in mind what goals you would like to achieve, whether it's an easier-to-navigate kitchen, an archive system for your collections, or a clutter-free desktop.

An organizer will typically make a preliminary visit to your home to get an idea of the job and discuss the time it will take and how much it will cost. Some will charge for this initial visit and some will not, so inquire in advance. Organizers will ask what seem like very personal questions, but they're not being nosy, they just want to learn about your organizational habits (or lack thereof). Be prepared to discuss what kind of results you hope to get out of their services. And keep in mind that the relationship with an organizer will be a very personal one—after all, you'll be rummaging through your belongings together—so good chemistry is key. Don't hire any organizer, no matter how good his or her references, if you cannot envision a relaxed, confident working relationship with that person.

You might not be able to make sense of all your possessions, but it's exactly their objectivity as outside observers that will allow professional organizers to identify the problems clearly. Organizers can pinpoint where there's a lack of storage, and whether or not more storage is a possibility. They will also help you figure out how to use the storage most efficiently. What about the dreaded process of getting rid of stuff? A good professional organizer will not force you to discard anything you don't want to do. They'll ask when was the last time you used an item? Is the item still useful and in good working condition? Is it something that you love? Is there a logical place for it somewhere in the home? And finally, rest assured that the best organizational makeovers aren't about teaching you tedious new tricks. If an organizer has done the job well, the system will be something you can easily stick to.

When you don't have room for a separate living room and den, and you would rather stow the television out of sight when you have guests, an armoire can hide it all away. Indeed, this one is large enough to conceal an entire media center, and it contributes to the room's streamlined look. Note how a rough-hewn barrel in the same honey color as the armoire unifies the look—and holds plenty of firewood.

OPPOSITE: A worn white cupboard found at a flea market brings an unexpected charm to this whitewashed living room. With the door closed, the space is a pleasant sitting room. Door open, it becomes the home's entertainment center. A large coffee table suits the overstuffed sofas and provides more surface for display.

RIGHT: Built-in shelving is always welcome. A library of books captures our imagination, and their varied sizes and colors create eye-catching displays. These volumes—a collection of design and gardening books—have been stacked on their sides, creating a clean overall presentation. This is an excellent way to store antique and large-format books, as storing them flat helps preserve their spines

BELOW: Fireplace accessories sometimes are made from objects never intended for that use. Here, a sturdy vintage colander with the patina of age holds extra logs. Though a small touch, its very subtlety lends a lot of style.

MEASURE FIRST Before building bookshelves, be sure to estimate how much space you'll need to hold your collection. For each linear foot of shelving, estimate eight to ten average-sized hardcovers (such as novels) or six to eight large hardcovers (such as reference works). Adjust the numbers slightly for especially thin or thick volumes.

CHAPTER TWO kitchens

perhaps more

than any other room, the kitchen inspires dreams of perfection. You might not have considered what your ideal bedroom would look like, but chances are you've got at least a few strong opinions about what for many is the heart of the home, the command center of family life, and the locus of many evenings of entertaining. Maybe it's time for a renovation, in which case, take careful notes about what you like about your kitchen and what you want to change. Start gathering photos and swatches for inspiration, but don't dismiss the possibility of getting closer to that dream kitchen even if you are not planning a large-scale overhaul. In the kitchen, small changes can have a big impact: A slight reorganizing that takes your habits into consideration will make it a joy to put things away—maybe that cabinet you dip into nineteen times a day could have its doors replaced by a curtain, which, beside providing easier access, could bring a new pattern into the space. Why not retrieve treasured collectibles from the depths of the cabinets (were they tucked

The Shaker philosophy of simple design is evident in this spacious kitchen, especially in the custom-built cabinetry. The cupboard and chest of drawers built into the corner of this kitchen provide ample room to ensure the proverbial place for everything. In addition to opening up cupboard space, hanging a pot rack overhead is an especially good option when you want to draw attention to a gorgeous ceiling, like this original wooden example with exposed beams. In a room this spare you have maximum freedom with what you want to leave out on the counter—a stainless-steel bread box and crocks of cooking utensils keep the essentials of daily living within reach and contribute to the kitchen's character.

back there for safekeeping?) and put them on display?
You'll enjoy looking at them every day, and you might even
remember to use them a little more often. If your kitchen lacks
character and you've always been more fond of your dishes
than of your cabinetry, consider replacing your overhead
storage with open shelving, a big change that costs pennies.
And in a real space crunch, a reframing of the question can
provide the answer: How to store your great big bowl
collection? Maybe it's time for the bowls themselves to become
their own original sort of storage.

The advantage of open shelving is
that it provides an opportunity to create
a display. This enormous island was
designed for cooking on one side and
table setting on the other. China,
glassware, and other kitchen items are
artfully arranged with cookbooks,
baskets, and table linens. A marriage of
storage and display, the objects are so
much more attractive than looking at
the back of a closed island.

OPEN SHELVES Open shelves work well in small kitchens because they can be tucked into corners and don't need additional space for a cabinet door to swing out.

LEFT & OPPOSITE: Cool hues of white, stainless steel, and blue give this kitchen a clean look, but it's the open shelving with china and glasses on display that lends it charm. Note how similar objects are grouped together: This renders every cubby its own work of art and also makes putting things away a snap. A mounted bar above the sink is a place to hang utensils, and wire stacking shelves on the countertops make neat room for extra bowls, dishes, and glassware.

A simple solution to kitchen storage is a hanging pot rack. The owner of this one dressed hers up with enormous red crepe-paper flowers, softening its industrial feel and echoing the red cookware. Custom cabinets with glass-front doors showcase her wedding china and vintage ceramics. A built-in wine rack keeps favorite vintages, bottled water, and other beverages at hand. Everything here is useful and welcoming—even an extra peninsula of storage cabinetry is set up to be a breakfast bar or a place for guests to sip their cocktails as the finishing touches are put on dinner.

OPPOSITE: While renovating their home, the homeowners decided to simplify the kitchen and opted for an unfitted style, which was more in keeping with the rural origins of the house. It's also easy to maintain. For storage, the couple selected wicker baskets that can be tucked away on shelves when not needed, or, in the case of large-scale baskets, under a worktable.

ABOVE LEFT: Here's a house-warming alternative to the same old spice rack from the kitchen store: A cast-off dollhouse mounted on the wall is home, sweet home for all those little jars. One this small could also work nicely on a kitchen countertop.

ABOVE RIGHT: An old ladder recycled as an overhead pot rack brings farmhouse charm to the kitchen. Eye-bolts allow you to mount it from the ceiling with chains; cup hooks in the rails hold lightweight saucepans and utensils, while S-hooks suspended from heavy-gauge wire wrapped around the rungs hold weightier pots and colanders. But this is no job for a debilitated ladder—be sure the wood is still sturdy enough to hold your cookware before installing.

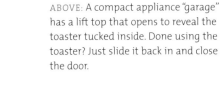

ABOVE: A compact appliance "garage" has a lift top that opens to reveal the toaster tucked inside. Done using the toaster? Just slide it back in and close the door.

LEFT: When you imagine this kitchen stripped down to its bare bones, with only the appliances and built-ins remaining in place, you can see that every ounce of its unpretentious style comes from the arrangement of the homeowner's possessions. Cupboard doors were removed in favor of open shelving. Each shelf has its own brand of organization to give the overall look one of order rather than clutter. In one cubby are easy-to-find ingredients in glass jars, and in another, drinking glasses. Underneath the industrial butcher-block island in the center of the room are fresh table linens, and dish towels are stacked and ready to go. Aluminum trash cans are perfect for storing dog or cat food.

Straight from the factory doesn't have to mean devoid of personality, as seen here with these two large shelving units fitted with metal baskets. Originally from a factory but purchased at an antiques market, the shelves and baskets are just as functional as a traditional hutch. The baskets are ideal for holding cutlery, table linens, and candles, everything necessary for a well-stocked kitchen. The stacked china warms the storage pieces. Stainless-steel shelves next to the window came from a restaurant supply store. The narrow stack of lockers—a nifty storage solution that would work in a bathroom as well—was also purchased at an antiques fair and conceals cleaning supplies. Found on the cheap, the industrial items give the kitchen a delightful and unexpected personality.

OPPOSITE: Brimming with flea-market finds, this kitchen is a wonderful example of resourcefulness. All the cabinets were found at flea markets and antiques shops. The mismatched lower cabinets were topped with new butcher-block countertops, and one was retrofitted to house a dishwasher (on the far right). A vintage tablecloth acts as a skirt, hiding cleaning supplies or a garbage bin behind it. The small shelf running across the window holds a favorite tea set that also doubles as an occasional collection of flower vases. On the countertops, glass jars keep baking ingredients fresh and an old-fashioned bread box does the same for bread. Additional bread boxes stacked above the cabinet provide more storage for items that don't need to be easily accessed.

ABOVE: A touch of modernity in the form of restaurant supply shelves does appear in this romantic, charm-infused kitchen. The shelves provide more storage for canisters, teacups, and paper towels.

RIGHT: The charm of the upper cabinets was enhanced by tacking lacy organza napkins inside the bottom panes of the glass-front doors. A trio of nesting bowls add vintage charm and storage for fruit.

Old-fashioned plate racks safeguard and display a collection of English ceramic ware. Plate racks are a classic country storage solution, keeping dishes at-the-ready and on view, a plus if you own a pretty collection. The kitchen island's deep drawers are reminiscent of bins found in a general store, a great option for storing pots and pans. Wide-mouth glass jars hold an array of sweets: candy canes, orange jellies, cookies, and marshmallows.

57

OPPOSITE: A stainless steel dowel above the stove is an idea borrowed from a professional kitchen that works perfectly in home kitchens, too. Clutter is kept to a minimum in this cozy yet streamlined kitchen, where everything is within reach. A pot rack keeps pots and pans at your fingertips. Note the two narrow shelves: one installed underneath the cabinet and another just above the range—they're small innovations that add a few inches of valuable space. Glass-fronted cabinets display colorful pottery.

Reinvent It

Be creative when scouting flea markets or garage sales for kitchen storage. Here, a former retail clothing rack has been given a new life as a whimsical place to hang pots and pans.

RIGHT: Everything about this quaint kitchen calls to mind a summer beach cottage. A cast-off vintage plant stand has been put to work storing plates and bowls. The narrow shelf above the counter and the under-the-cabinet rack for stemware make the most of a tight space and keep attractive glassware in view. A space-saving rack organizes pots and pans on the side of the cabinets, and an iron bar mounted on the side of the counter is perfect for dish towels. And most charming of all, a small magnetic strip holds a colorful collection of vintage spreaders.

The great room in this weekend camp-style home is divided into living, dining, and cooking areas. Storage was built into the design, with the goal of keeping it simple. The galley kitchen is compact but contains an ample amount of storage. A custom-built dish rack fits perfectly into a niche between the solid-door cabinets, keeping frequently used dinnerware immediately accessible. The long kitchen island has drawers for pots and pans, serving ware, and other kitchen necessities.

OPPOSITE: The extraordinary appeal of this kitchen comes from the elegant simplicity of its storage. Even the closed storage has an open feel. The glass doors allow green dishware to add an accent color to the room, one that's echoed in the mint-green blender. Inspired by kitchen galley storage on a boat, a stainless-steel rod running along the bottom of the open shelf is a measure of protection against reaching for a glass and knocking others over. Below, standing in for traditional cabinets, are glass-front drawers deep enough for large pots and pans. Glass-front cabinets and drawers are practical—they make it easy to find what you're looking for.

RIGHT: Cabinetry can be expensive—and difficult to plan in small kitchens, because it can visually dominate the room without contributing anything extra in style. But this dainty kitchen illustrates how great style can be had on a shoestring budget by dispensing with traditional upper cabinets. Exposed shelving, mounted on iron brackets and painted jade green to match the vintage bowls and Depression glass, runs around the perimeter of the room. Cup hooks underneath the shelves create additional space to store mugs and teacups. Vintage swing-out towel bars above the sink are a logical solution for damp towels, and they can be folded against the wall when not in use. The lower cabinets, painted with a light green wash and fitted with vintage knobs, underscore the retro look of the shelves and glassware.

storing fine tableware

whether handed down from grandparents or unearthed at flea markets, china, crystal, and silverware make strong statements when left on display or presented at the table—but require careful handling to help them last for the next generation. Here are some tips for taking care of these pieces, as well as enjoying them regularly.

- Whether displaying china, crystal, or silver, or storing it in a cupboard, it should be washed at least once a year. Despite their impervious looks, these materials are porous, so dust can penetrate and dull their appearance over time. To avoid streaking, dry with a lint-free cloth.

- Even in the case of tall, delicate items, such as Champagne flutes or candelabra, always store pieces right-side up. Rims, ears, and arms are always more fragile, since they weren't designed to bear weight, and laying items on their sides, even if well-padded, can strain and weaken them. If boxing them up for the attic, use padded containers and wrap each item individually. Use cardboard dividers as tall as the box so that they support the lid, should anything fall onto the box.

- When stacking precious plates or bowls, slip a round of felt or even paper plates between them to prevent their feet from scratching the glaze on the dishes beneath them.

- Washing silver thoroughly and hand drying before putting it away will prevent tarnish; do not wrap in latex, wool, or felt, as these will cause silver to tarnish more quickly. Do not store silver in the basement, as high humidity can speed tarnishing. Do not toss silver flatware into a box or drawer where they might rattle around; invest in a wooden case, preferably lined with tarnish-resistant cloth.

- Hand washing is always best, but take care to line your sink with a rubber pad or cloth, keep the spigot turned away from where you're washing to prevent scratching or breakage, and remove all rings and bracelets before handling.

Open shelving doesn't have to mean a very informal look. Dark stained wood and a collection of fine china give this room a sophisticated air. A plate rack above the sink stores dishes, and the tile backsplash echoes the feel of the china collection. Rarely used platters are kept high, but cups hang on low hooks.

ABOVE: An old steel cabinet cleans up nicely with fresh butcher block on top and casters affixed below. Besides the work surface, drawers, and cupboards gained, it also gives the kitchen great character. The rest of the room is kept rustic: A two-tiered wooden dish rack puts the china on display, and a narrow shelf above the counter adds a bit more storage for a collection of favorite bowls.

RIGHT: A quirky mix of retro, rainbow, and even hardware-store chic characterizes this kitchen, inhabited by the owner of an antiques shop. The unique pieces, like the hardware cabinet fitted with crystal knobs, create lots of storage space, but many objects are included just for their aesthetic charm. An enormous garden urn is a humorous response to ubiquitous unadorned utensil crocks.

OPPOSITE: Industrial elements mix easily with wood, stone, and leather in this compact but highly functional galley kitchen. A sturdy steel meat rack has been converted into a pot rack and attached to an antique butcher-block table, becoming the focal point of the kitchen area as well as storage for pots, pans, and other kitchen accoutrements. A metal rack underneath holds tomatoes, keeping them at room temperature. A basket off to the side is big enough to work as a garbage or recycling bin.

MORE CUPBOARD SPACE Hanging pots and pans from an overhead rack frees up cupboard space and provides a focal point for the kitchen.

ABOVE: A butler's pantry is a service room usually placed between the kitchen and dining room. It functions as a place to store table linens, serving platters, bar ware, and additional china pieces and also as a staging area for formal dining and entertaining. This butler's pantry is neatly fitted with cabinets that provide ample storage space, including drawers, cabinets, and a wine cooler. With bar necessities, a sink, and a dishwasher this one serves its purpose beautifully.

LEFT: Collections stored on open shelves become the center of attention and are easily accessed. Here, long wooden shelves that wrap around the interior of the kitchen create plenty of room for an array of vintage cake plates, pitchers, dishes, and bowls, showcasing the collections' many shades of white. Ironstone pitchers elegantly display kitchen utensils, grouped by material (wood with wood, metal with metal). A wire milk crate contains table linens and flatware; since it can be carried right to the table; arranging place settings has never been easier.

QUICK CHANGE

By removing your upper kitchen cabinets and replacing them with open shelves, you can create a budget-friendly, highly functional, and casually chic new look for your kitchen. Open shelves create a focal point, in addition to putting your dishes at your fingertips.

LEFT: A small butler's pantry off the kitchen does its part, housing a butcher block counter, microwave, and dishwasher, as well as a Harlequin dish collection that's really meant to be on display (hooks mounted onto wraparound molding maximize every inch of space). At dinnertime, folding French doors hide the work space.

In lieu of pricey kitchen cabinets, let flea-market finds do the trick. The farm sink was assembled from an old sideboard, a salvage-yard marble slab, and a basic soapstone potting-shed sink. Above the refrigerator, former balusters act as dividers for cookie sheets, cutting boards, and platters. An old garden gate has been transformed into an overhead pot rack by suspending it from the ceiling.

If you find the casual charm of glass cabinet doors appealing but still prefer concealed storage, opt for glass doors fitted with curtains. These cabinets feature ticking-inspired striped curtains, which give them a tailored look, but other patterns, such as a floral or Provençal motif, will work, or even a solid color. New hardware was also installed, a minor change that is quick and easy to make and can result in a fresh, new look.

PICTURE PERFECT If the interior of your pantry will be on view, you'll want to keep the contents looking orderly. Place pastas, beans, flour, and sugar into matching glass jars for a streamlined look.

ABOVE: Two more space-saving additions: a pocket door and a cabinet between two doorways.

ABOVE: In older homes, you'll commonly find a pantry off the kitchen rather than a battery of cabinets, and it can be just as charming and useful as ever. Connecting it to the kitchen with a screen door opens up the room a bit more than a solid door, allows air to circulate, and lets you see the contents at a glance.

Outdated hanging cabinets were replaced by inexpensive painted shelves in this classic kitchen. The shelves contribute to the room's sense of openness. The top shelf is dedicated to displaying favorite objects. Instead of replacing the two schoolhouse-style lamps above the island with a pot rack, the homeowner opted to take advantage of some open space at the right to hang a small pot rack.

LEFT: Replacing your cabinet doors is a terrific way to make a quick-and-easy change to your kitchen storage. Here, louvered cabinet doors add style and call to mind the shutters on an old house. The nautical theme struck by the wicker and wood in white, blue, and natural brown is carried to its logical end by its sheer tidiness—china is out on open shelves, but symmetry
in the arrangements makes the small spaces appear neat as a pin.

OPPOSITE: Dishes can be reached in an instant in this informal kitchen in a beach cottage. Open shelves set between wall studs hold glasses and stemware for entertaining family and friends, as well as plates, cookbooks, teapots, and other kitchen necessities. A skirt under the sink is ideal for concealing cleaning supplies and a garbage can.

BELOW: Craftsman-style open shelving enhances the kitchen's airy, informal feeling—and allows plenty of space for both storage and display. It's the perfect stage for those unique pieces with pretty shapes, such as cake stands, creamers, and bowls, to shine. On the counter, canisters hold staples, and an elegant white platter gleams on a small shelf installed above the backsplash.

ABOVE: Here, all the comforts of a modern kitchen combine with the look of an old-fashioned one. Take the dishwasher, for example, which, clad in the same wood as the cabinetry, disappears completely. There's plenty of drawer space for smaller things, thanks to the cabinet that extends all the way down to the countertop. Closing in the area this way is not only practical; it makes the space much cozier.

BELOW: A cast-off set of drawers was fitted with a sink and reinvented as kitchen furniture. A tile counter and backsplash complete the makeover. Beaded board on the dishwasher replaces a plain Plexiglass panel. Painted the same color as the former bureau, it fits right in. A plate rack holds dishware, and a small shelf unit keeps stemware in order. Baskets and hooks fulfill the rest of the kitchen's storage needs.

ABOVE: If you, like this kitchen's owner, have ever been captivated by a certain kind of collectible—say, mustard-yellow mugs and mixing bowls—you know the temptation of planning a whole kitchen around it. This can be a very positive impulse, as evidenced by the golden coat on these cabinets. The deeper shade of yellow supports the collection and creates the reason to bring out those beloved pieces from behind cabinet doors.

ABOVE: Whether frequent entertainers or parents of teenagers, you'll be pleased with the installation of a cooling drawer, a small refrigerator hidden among your cabinetry, designed for beverages. Beside freeing space in the fridge, it allows guests to help themselves without having to venture into the cook's domain.

ABOVE: A gorgeous old French laundry basket mounted on casters is a beautiful match for the space beneath this counter. Whether you use it to hold table linens or to collect recycling, the wheels ensure smooth transport to the garage or laundry room.

ABOVE: A wall-mounted basket corrals handy but oddly shaped kitchen tools, like a cheese grater and a pie slicer. A magnetic knife bar keeps your knives all in one place and protects their blades from contact with other utensils. Underneath the counter, a thick blue curtain mounted on a sliding track conceals deep shelving that is just right for large pots.

RIGHT: You can purchase utensil crocks in every kitchen store, but improvising has its rewards. Throw open your cupboards and cast an eye on those beloved finds that might not get as much use as you would like—the antique copper pot? The McCoy pitcher? Or maybe even think outside the kitchen. Here, a garden urn does the job with elegance.

OPPOSITE: Updating your kitchen doesn't have to mean giving the whole room a face-lift. Remove several strategically chosen cabinet doors along with their hardware, and suddenly you've created variety in look and function. Baskets turn the spaces into improvised drawers, while the interruption in continuity gives the kitchen a new relaxed personality.

ABOVE & RIGHT: Putting china on display in glass-front cabinets is often pretty enough, but the arresting use of color in this kitchen shows how attractive cabinets can provide a backdrop for china that truly enhances its charm. An easy way to freshen up aging cabinets is to paint the interior a different color, which draws attention to the items displayed inside.

EASY VISIBILITY Glass-front cabinets allow you to easily identify the contents. They also place collections of china and glassware on display, but protect them from dust and accidents.

ABOVE: A wooden china cabinet would normally be the pride of the dining room. But with a weathered white finish, it can step gracefully into any kitchen, creating instant storage. Despite its relatively small dimensions—you can tuck it right into a corner—this piece of furniture holds a lot. Fine dishes and silver pieces are safe behind its doors, while heavier ironstone is grouped on top to show it off. Drawers are wide enough to accommodate lots of silverware and table linens.

ABOVE: Utilitarian though it may be, the pantry can be as attractive as any other part of the house. The key is careful organization and a few personal touches. Much of the appeal of this charming pantry is the arrangement of the contents on its shelves. Rather than organize a riot of unattractive supermarket packaging, transfer the contents of pasta boxes, flour bags, and other staples into jars of a uniform size; stash larger items in catch-all baskets (lining with fabric is a nice touch, as they can be easily laundered). Old recipe boxes, antique canisters, and kitchen tools add charm.

countertops: what to leave out, what to put away

just as you might spend hours choosing the right tile for the backsplash or finding the perfect shade of paint for your kitchen walls, you would do well to put as much effort into considering what you should store on your kitchen countertops—and what you should not. These surfaces fall squarely into that hazy area between utilitarian and decorative, and generally, a mix of often-used appliances and decorative items lives here. But striking the right balance is key: Too much stuff on the counter looks cluttered and gets in the way of cooking; too little appears cold and can turn everyday tasks, like making breakfast, into drudgery.

Resist the temptation to fill your largest expanse of countertop with objects. Instead, leave this area clear for a work space—ideally, a large enough space for a cutting board, for rolling dough, and for prep bowls or a pot pulled off the stove. Take advantage of awkward corners or smaller stretches of the countertop as places for appliances and display.

Arrange items on the counters in clusters: Canisters of baking staples should be grouped together, as should appliances used in tandem—a toaster and the coffee maker, both used in the morning, would be most convenient if placed near each other. Transfer oils and vinegars from their large bottles into smaller containers that are better looking when left out and store the rest in a cool, dark place.

Finally, consider the style statement you'd like to make. If all your appliances happen to be cherry red, leaving them out in a kitchen that strives for retro appeal will enhance the overall look. However, if your appliances are mismatched or unattractive, you might stow them away and supplement the kitchen's style with some favorite collectibles: mixing bowls as a home for onions, garlic, potatoes, and fruit; a display of teacups; or several beloved pitchers used as utensil crocks.

Beautiful leaded-glass doors add Old World elegance to this compact kitchen. Storage in the rest of the room is well-planned, too. Besides the many cabinets, books get their own cubby, and a metal rack both stores and displays a collection of platters

LEFT: A renovation afforded an avid cook her dream, not only in the fridge and freezer, but in the built-in bookshelves that frame them. Bookshelves can be constructed in all sorts of nooks and crannies, or they can wrap or fill any wall in the kitchen. Another creative addition: a Victorian screen door opening to the pantry graces the room with its one-of-a-kind charm.

RIGHT: This setup combines the sleek touches of a restaurant kitchen with the relaxed, lived-in feel of a home. China on exposed shelves are a bit of both, as pitchers up above lend their lovely lines to the room, while dishes lower down can be grabbed easily as soon as dinner's ready. Stainless-steel accessories echo the appliances, and a marble countertop is gorgeous, as well as the baker's best friend. When the pass-through isn't needed for "service," an enticing bowl of fruit will still draw the eye in its direction.

This galley kitchen is filled with storage solutions. Within one kitchen are two examples of the two-for-one: a rack installed inside the door of this under-the-sink cabinet takes advantage of its depth. A bucket and larger bottles and supplies tuck easily right into the cabinet, while smaller items can be kept together in the rack, keeping you from having to root around in the back for bottles and cans that go missing. In the flatware drawer, a second sliding rack atop the existing one doubles the space. A shallow peg rail takes advantage of the wall space.

5 great ideas from this room

1 Salvaged cabinets from the 1920s were renovated with new marble countertops.

2 An old-fashioned step-back hutch fits right in with the kitchen's farmhouse style.

3 The pot rack eliminates the need for more cabinets to hold pots and pans, and, with the table-turned-kitchen-island, acts as a focal point in the room.

4 Old church pews painted a creamy white were put to use as a showcase for serving platters and trays.

5 Creative storage adds fun to stowing the basics—a vintage baby crib holds a basket of fresh produce.

With limited space for upper cabinets, multiple drawers help maximize storage in this kitchen. A plate rack keeps blue-and-white china within reach. The island doubles as a table, and also offers storage for cookbooks and additional china. A small recess above one of the few cabinets is the perfect place to display a collection of yellowware bowls, and narrow glass-front cabinets on each side of the stove alcove hold glasses and stemware. A narrow ledge above the alcove supports a quartet of plates

CHAPTER THREE bathrooms

we all start our day in the bathroom, often still only semiconscious, and not always ready for the day ahead. Thus, a serene setting and intuitive organization here are crucial—a challenge since the bathroom is chock full of little things that need homes. Perhaps because we think of it as a utilitarian space, a very common underestimation of the bathroom is to work with what's there, rather than seeing what could be possible. In this relatively small room, bringing in just one piece of furniture, or one personal piece of art, can mean the difference between a haphazard room and one that looks pulled together. Instead of viewing it as a random grouping of toilet, tub, and sink, cast an eye on the spaces between those fixtures. Is there a gap somewhere that doesn't really need to remain empty—in fact, that would feel a lot cozier if it were filled? Is there bare wall space where a bit more shelving would help, or even provide room for some beloved object that would make the bathroom homier and more inviting?

A special find calls for special treatment: the owners of this Long Island beach cottage discovered a 300-year-old marble basin from Turkey, which they had wall-mounted and fitted as a sink. A vanity chest fit perfectly underneath. The sink's metal supports double as towel bars; everything else is kept sleek and spare to show off the antique basin to best effect.

Baskets and bins can help make sense of the smaller things. In this most pared down of rooms, a little softness in the form of something delightfully unnecessary—just there to exist as an eye pleaser—whether a bunch of fresh-cut flowers, a beautiful print, a crystal light fixture from the flea market, or some framed family photos, can go a long way toward warming up all that tile.

ABOVE: Twin surface-mounted sinks fitted with fabric skirts create concealed storage where none existed. The fabric skirts give you the flexibility to keep unattractive items from view, while adding old-fashioned charm.

LEFT: Instead of a conventional sink unit, which can feel blocky in the wrong setting, or a pedestal sink, which is elegant but lacks storage, the simple open shelving beneath this sink offers options galore. Supplemental shelving on the side means plenty of room for personal items. Plush towels and a pretty basket infuse the space with a spa atmosphere.

The homeowners' affection for Shaker design is evident in this cottage's master bathroom. The furniture-style cabinetry lines are classic, providing plenty of open and closed storage for towels, toiletries, and decorative items.

OPPOSITE & RIGHT: Tucked into a gable, this guest bathroom inspired creative thinking when it came to storage. A cast-off nightstand topped with a silver tray for shaving supplies offers both storage and personality. The small corner shelf along the side of the shower provides a place to put soap and shampoo, while open shelving and an under-table basket make it easy for guests to find fresh towels.

ADVANCE PLANNING

When designing a bathroom that's to be furnished with freestanding storage pieces, be sure to have all the components and their dimensions in advance before finalizing the plans with your contractor. He or she will need to include any quirky pieces in the plans before beginning work.

5 great ideas from this room

1 Antiques can be incorporated into any room of the house. Here, an old hanging cupboard reflects the homeowners' love of antiques and keeps an ample supply of towels at the ready.

2 New fixtures were matched to old: The vanity was custom-made to match the wainscoting on the walls.

3 A peg rail provides a place for hanging towels and bathrobes. Note that it's set directly above the radiator, which warms the towels on chilly mornings.

4 Items traditionally meant for other rooms or uses can be put to work elsewhere: A rustic green picnic basket is ideal for corralling small toiletries in one place.

5 Makeup brushes, cotton balls, and toothbrushes are stored in pretty containers. Any other supplies, especially those in unattractive containers, are kept hidden from view under the sink.

OPPOSITE: A fully upholstered spot for lounging in the bathroom is a comfortable extra, but it also makes great sense when it does double-duty as a storage trunk. Two kitchen carts under the window hold towels, toiletries, and plants; bath products in sleek bottles that maintain the colors of the bathroom are pleasing to the eye.

RIGHT: Though it's a tight spot between the chair and the window, a small armoire can deftly squeeze in and be all the storage you need in a bathroom. Charmingly distressed, this one holds a little bit of everything—a television and radio, extra blankets and towels, and some decorative pieces from the china cabinet—all of which easily can be hidden away behind closed doors when not in use or when visitors drop in.

pretty bottles and canisters

the lovelier the bathroom, the more glaring the bottle of shampoo with the garish label that announces, "Now, 30% more FREE!" After putting so much effort into creating a bathroom that is beautiful, comfortable, and well-organized, you don't want ugly packaging to spoil the effect. Instead, consider this decorator's trick that might seem fussy at first, but which will make your life easier and go miles toward achieving great style. Decanting soaps, shampoos, and other toiletries into pretty containers will make them disappear from view, conform to the bathroom's décor, or contribute lively splashes of color, depending on your preference. And in this day and age of buying in bulk, it's a practical solution as well. Opaque pump bottles in stainless steel or ceramic can be purchased inexpensively in home stores; or, in a very spare bathroom that you'd like to enliven with color, the saturated hues of many shampoos and hand soaps will look great shining through clear plastic bottles. Unless your toiletries are nicely packaged, store any large or unattractive containers under the sink or in a closed cabinet, and arrange the rest around the tub, on the counter, or on exposed shelves. You'll be a believer as soon as you notice that it's not all those good-looking containers you see, but just a gorgeous bathroom.

Intending to create a one-of-a-kind master bath for her circa 1800 farmhouse, this homeowner set out to find components with an Old World feel. She found a $50 mahogany-veneered dresser with good bones and transformed it into an elegant vanity with several coats of paint topped with crackle medium, a marble top, and two undermounted porcelain sinks. Shapely containers on a silver tray make elegant packaging for toiletries.

OPPOSITE: Starting from scratch offers limitless possibilities to set a one-of-a-kind tone in a bathroom. This one uses materials familiar to farmers—galvanized steel washbasins for a sink and a tub. The vanity was designed to look like a chicken coop. But beside its whimsical touch, the chicken wire actually has a practical function, allowing air to circulate through the cabinets. A stool acts as a shower caddy, holding soap and a towel. Fresh flowers and a few personal items on display ensure that this bathroom is as warm and welcoming as can be.

TAKE IT WITH YOU

Freestanding bathroom storage, unlike built-in, can be moved with you when you relocate to a new house.

ABOVE: Industrial chic, in the form of metal furniture paired with exposed brick, is at its cozy best in this attic-turned-master-suite. A vintage green metal dresser sets the tone for the whole room. A medicine cabinet on casters creates a countertop next to the sink, and a steel-framed mirror carries the mid-century theme.

Reinvent It

Antiques and collectibles can be called into service in new roles, as seen by these vintage gym-locker baskets. Affixed to the wall, they're put to work as cubbies for soap, towels, and even spare slippers.

LEFT: The freestanding cabinet is a replica of an early-twentieth-century physician's cabinet, and keeps a basket of toiletries, supplies, and fresh towels in view. Its glass walls let light from the sunny window shine through, eliminating any feeling of visual clutter that a solid piece might contribute. A chair functions as an additional perch for towels or a robe. Perhaps best of all, this bathroom reflects the idea that personal touches go a long way in tying it all together—with a botanical print on the wall and potted orchid on the edge of the tub.

ABOVE: Little bits of luxury can also contribute to superb storage: A silver trophy cup for makeup brushes and a miniature vase in black Wedgwood jasperware for cotton balls keep essentials shipshape in an artful way.

BELOW: Quirky details, such as the wire glove forms and small whisk brooms, turn this small bathroom into one with a sense of fun. A narrow shelf installed under the mirror supplies additional storage space by supporting silver cups that keep cotton swabs, toothbrushes, and other small essentials in order; even the aspirin is transferred to an antique glass medicine bottle with a metal cap.

SMALL SPACE IDEA
Installing a narrow shelf underneath the bathroom mirror adds more space to set pretty containers filled with cotton balls, swabs, and other essentials.

ABOVE: A lack of built-in cabinetry calls for creative thinking. This bathroom was given instant glamour with a charming armoire fronted with chicken wire—which lets the contents breathe, a big plus in a humid room—and painted a bright shade of blue. Though it's roomy enough to hold virtually all bathroom needs, the two visible shelves are outfitted with extra care: fluffy towels are stacked on the top, and the attractive canisters and apothecary jars for storing supplies make the middle shelf a pretty focal point.

When dealing with a tight space, think about every cranny to maximize storage. For this bathroom, the answer to extra towel storage lay beyond its walls in the form of recessed cubby shelving and drawers. A basket on the floor next to the tub keeps towels within reach, and since they are next to the radiator, warms them on cold days.

CONSIDER A DRESSER
Any piece of furniture, especially a dresser with nice lines, that is large enough to accommodate a sink can be adapted to become a vanity unit.

BELOW: Open shelves work in the bathroom just as well as in the kitchen—here, they hold extra towels close at hand. A French Provincial buffet was stripped, painted, and modified to hold two sinks. Bringing lovely cherished objects—fresh flower arrangements, family photos, or a painting—into the bathroom draws attention away from utilitarian details, such as a chrome towel bar.

ABOVE: Even though its traditional location is over the sink, a vintage medicine chest, especially when it's an eye-catching one-of-a-kind, will look just right in another spot on the wall. Here, it not only provides additional storage for toiletries, but also functions as hung art, injecting a big hit of character to a small space.

flea market style

There's no limit to the types of flea market finds that can make organizing your medicine chest, bathroom cabinets, and countertop a pleasure. Refrigerator boxes, antique medicine jars, small silver cups or pottery, and even items from other rooms of the house—think tiny flower pots, collectible tins, little creamers and sugar bowls—can fit those tight spaces.

The medicine chest is often the room's smallest space, but also the most important, as it's used on a daily basis. Limit its contents to toiletries, not bathroom cleaners; this is also not the place for anything used less frequently than once a week. Decant liquids from large containers, like mouthwash or body lotion, into smaller, lidded jars or antique bottles; transfer small quantities of cotton balls or swabs into teacups, diminutive vases, or juice glasses, and stash the rest under the sink in its original packaging. Every few weeks, refill all the containers, and remove anything that has landed here, but is not part of your daily or weekly routines.

Cabinets can benefit from planning and editing, too. Group like with like, keeping all your makeup together in one place, all medicines and home remedies in another; ideally, each will have its own shelf or drawer. Small baskets can make these spaces easier to use, converting high shelves into drawers you can pull out or dividing large spaces into more manageable ones. Under the sink, group all cleaning products together and bulk packages together; arrange them in low, wide containers or trays that keep them upright and are easy to pull out and locate what you are looking for.

Finally, consider what you'll keep on the countertop. Though these items can certainly be utilitarian, say, if you like to keep your makeup brushes or moisturizer on hand, keep in mind that they will contribute to the look of the room; choose vessels accordingly and transfer soaps and other products from their packaging to pretty bottles and trays.

Four charming and easy-to-implement storage ideas infuse this old-fashioned bathroom (note the separate faucets for hot and cold water) with all the comforts of the modern day without succumbing to any of the latest fads. A slender shelf topping the wall paneling is perfect for toiletries, candles, and two shapely pitchers. An antique wall-mounted medicine chest is just as spacious as any purchased from a home improvement store. Ticking-stripe toiletry bags suspended from a peg rail add timeless charm, and a flower pail is an ideal container for long-handled back scrub brushes.

Timeless materials such as marble and wood give this spacious master bath its opulence, but useful storage keeps it anchored in practicality as well. A cabinet and cubby over the toilet stores fluffy white towels and other necessities, while four white, wooden shelves over the tub hold vintage glass apothecary jars and bottles filled with scented soaps and bubble bath.

PRETTY SOAP STORAGE
Bath soaps stored in an attractive, open container make a lovely bathroom centerpiece and can subtly scent the room.

This vision in white illustrates how utility and beauty can be one and the same, especially when you have the luxury of custom storage in a large bathroom. Built-in open shelving with an elegant arched top provides ample space for storing towels, while baskets keep smaller items together, including a wire basket for loofahs. Such spaciousness allows you to create order and a visually appealing display: Towels can be interspersed with other objects that are simply pleasing to the eye. Throw your robe over the rocking chair or place your towel on its seat while you bathe—when called upon, it stands in for a hook. The overall effect is charming, but even better, convenient, as all your needs are effortlessly taken care of.

OPPOSITE: This luxurious setup shows why it pays to venture outside the bath department when shopping for bathroom furniture. A step-back cupboard loses its dining-room associations when filled with towels, and in fact, it balances the modern elements—the glassed-in shower and deep bathtub across the room. The mix of visible shelving above and closed cabinets below seems to make just as much sense in the bathroom as it does in the dining room; as in the dining room, keep your lovely items on the upper shelves, and stow the unattractive ones behind closed doors.

BELOW: The question of where to put towels is answered with pure luxury. A spa-inspired bathroom, sleek and modern down to its teak bathmat, wouldn't be complete without these warming drawers for keeping towels and bathrobes toasty. If you're renovating and would like to implement this idea in your own home, be sure to look for warming drawers specifically intended for the bathroom.

ABOVE: Clean lines give this modern bathroom a fresh, airy feel, but less apparent, its ample storage space contributes both serenity and order. A roomy Shaker-style vanity provides plenty of storage space for cleaning products and bath tissue; three drawers catch all the daily needs: cosmetics and soaps, medicines, and a blow-dryer. And for those items you always want within easy reach, a rustic bench next to the shower serves as a repository for extra towels, and a wire basket on the bench gathers the washcloths. Better still, the bench creates storage space beneath it, where baskets conceal additional toiletries.

CHAPTER FOUR bedrooms

talking about storage and the bedroom in the same breath initially seems contradictory; the former speaks of a chore, while the latter is ideally a deeply personal, restful haven. Yet having a place for everything is the key to achieving a truly relaxing and stylish bedroom. Keep in mind that one idea doesn't fit all—a deep armoire may feel heaven-sent in your room, but might be unsuitable for a young child, who'd be better off with a series of low cubbyholes that he'll love to fill with his toys. Tailoring furniture to each inhabitant's needs is what will ultimately personalize these rooms. Don't overlook the guest room— several empty drawers, easy access to spare blankets, and a few charming details that convey the style of the host are essential. It's not about keeping up appearances for those who visit, but about making each room more livable to the person who spends time in it, whether for a just few days or every night.

A bed without a footboard provides the opportunity to create your own visual anchor for the end of the bed. Here, it's two stacked baskets with scalloped cotton liners that can hold anything from magazines to spare slippers.

ABOVE: **Rather than add another chest of drawers** to an already full room, a collection of vintage steamer trunks and dome-topped chests, unified in look by their distressed leather and weathered hardware, can be a much more interesting choice. Stacked from largest to smallest, they are visually appealing and incredibly useful—these can handle a whole wardrobe of off-season clothing or extra blankets.

RIGHT: **Most farmhouses** were constructed with very little built-in storage, especially in the bedroom. In this farmhouse bedroom, a roomy Shaker-style armoire is a good solution for storing clothes, bed linens, and an extra blanket or two. Above the armoire, a set of hat boxes is both stylish and practical.

116

LEFT: In a cozy nook of the bedroom with a chair and ottoman for reading or napping, you barely notice the practical: a stack of vintage suitcases that not only provides a place to rest your book or a cup of tea, but is also as spacious inside as a small chest of drawers.

ABOVE: A place for everything, including a much-beloved collection of ribbed turtlenecks. This old oak wardrobe was rescued from a church basement. Fitted with shelves, it's the perfect repository for clothing that needs to be stored flat, and it makes an appealing visual display as well.

Reinvent It

Find creative uses for objects. Here, an old rake hangs on a door and organizes a mass of pretty necklaces.

RIGHT: This Shaker-inspired built-in combines the space-saving features of a closet with the divided drawers and cupboards that make dressers so useful. The upper cupboards can hold purses, sweaters, or a television, or they can be outfitted with a dowel to accommodate hanging jackets and shirts. The lower drawers, which increase in size nearer the floor, make organizing your clothing a breeze.

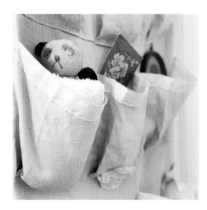

ABOVE & RIGHT: Ignore the intended purpose of a shoe caddy and put it to use for other storage. Sewn from linen and trimmed with old ribbon, this one is filled with mementos, and it is a comforting presence every time the closet door is opened. Shoe caddies are also ideal for storing belts, scarves, hair accessories, socks, and countless other small items. The table skirt is a perfect cover for items stored underneath it.

OPPOSITE: A peg rail is a smart addition in a bedroom, as there's always a place to hang a robe or a coat. But it also converts a hat collection into a decorating element that lends its own kind of character to the room. Vintage suitcases, stylish storage themselves, complement the look.

TUCK UNDERNEATH
Beds house one of the most overlooked sources of hidden storage: the space underneath. Under-bed storage keeps belongings neatly out of sight.

the versatility of armoires

if you've noticed a recurring theme in this book, it could be the use of armoires. Originally designed for holding weapons and fashioned with beautiful lines and Old World craftsmanship, antique armoires can be found at just about all types of antiques shops and flea markets. Since they were very popular as wardrobes when built-in closets were rare, many older armoires will have a compartment fitted with a rod for hanging clothing; adding shelving or drawers can update them for modern use. Armoires of all sizes can solve storage problems in just about any room of the house:

in the bedroom: Armoires still work beautifully as clothing or linen closets, or they can store a television and CD player.

in the kitchen: Use one as a breakfront to house china; those with glass-front doors will show off a collection, while solid doors will conceal.

in the bathroom: An armoire can make an all-in-one towel closet and toiletry hub.

in the office: Fit shelves with baskets to make them a pretty filing cabinet; convert the armoire itself into an office by extending one shelf with a fold-out setup for a desk.

in the living room or den: The armoire can conceal an entire entertainment unit; drill holes in the back for ventilation and to thread cords.

As any collector knows, storing quilts can be tricky: While their bulk usually demands that they be spread throughout the linen closets of the house, this huge armoire shows the lovely effect of keeping them together in one place. With their folds facing outward, they form a visual filing system of patterns—you can find just the one you're looking for in a single glance.

BELOW & RIGHT: **The master bedroom** in this 900-square-foot cottage (formerly a schoolhouse) lacked space for any freestanding storage, but the homeowners were able to turn this negative into a positive and maximize every inch of the small room by designing built-in storage in the awkward spaces under the eaves. The low-pitched roof created a seemingly unusable three-foot-high gap on each side of the room. A carpenter was hired to fill one side with bookshelves, and the other with cabinets and storage drawers to compensate for the lack of closet space.

ABOVE: In place of a traditional nightstand, two gorgeous stacked trunks stow bed linens and serve as a nightstand. Their soothing shades of brown fool the eye: These trunks are much larger than a standard nightstand, yet you don't perceive their great size, as they blend with the rest of the room.

ABOVE: For a girl who loves to play dress-up, this old-fashioned general store–type bin organizes her collection of accessories and other treasures. Labels keep things easy to find. On the wall, a shelf supports a stamp set and letters and an improvised clothespin photo holder displays snapshots or small works of art.

5 great ideas from this wardrobe

1 A model of efficiency, this custom-designed wardrobe does double duty—the other side functions as a headboard for the bed.

2 Pull-out wood trays keep smaller items such as socks, ties, and handkerchiefs in order and gathered together.

3 Deep drawers give the wardrobe a solid foundation visually and hold t-shirts, sweaters, athletic wear and other bulky clothes.

4 A distinctive touch, the antique industrial drawer pulls are stamped "1786."

5 A shelf installed toward the back of the wardrobe provides a second shelf for shoes.

ABOVE: Schools have long capitalized on the cozy appeal of cubbyholes, and indeed, they work for kids of all ages. Younger children love turning each cube into a sort of diorama with their toys, while older ones will appreciate having their favorite things so close at hand.

LEFT: A collection of Bakelite horse pins, old Navajo and Mexican silver, and a bevy of new and vintage belts play up the Western theme in this home. While one belt or pin may not catch the eye, when displayed together, their appeal is amplified. The crude construction of the cubby tool cabinet and its straightforward approach to keeping objects in order appealed to the homeowner's sense of practicality.

Many people don't invest much into the aesthetics of their closets since the space is not on display. We prefer the sensibility of this couple's walk-in; knowing that attractive surroundings feel more orderly and pleasant, they put effort and a sense of fun in every corner. Stenciling the walls with "his" and "hers" spells out whose belongings go where; note the impact of the wallpaper in what is generally a drab space. Invest in the finest shelving you can afford, because solid, quality shelving is worth its cost in both good looks and ease of maintenance. Boxes and bins function as drawers to customize the shelving even further.

planning a walk-in closet

every space in the house should feel good to you, including the closet.

Customizing your closet's hanging bars, drawers, shelves, and cubbyholes to fit your needs can make it feel as if you have doubled your storage space, but paying attention to the aesthetics of the closet will actually help it stay organized and easy-to-use for a long time. A lot of people ignore their closets or don't put much effort into their aesthetics, because closets are such utilitarian spaces. Paint the inside a stimulating color that you love, and since the clothing will hide most of it, don't be afraid to go bright; choose a glossy finish that will resist marks from hangers and will not rub off on clothing. Alternately, the closet is an excellent candidate for wallpaper that you might hesitate to use in a more visible part of the house.

Paring down your wardrobe is a good first step to planning the closet, and this should be done even before you design the layout. Consider the often-stated rule that if you haven't worn something in a year that you should get rid of it (although if you really love something, keep it), and be disciplined about whether an item deserves a spot in your new closet. The skirt you wear once a week? Of course, hold onto it. The one you try on once a week, then put back in the closet because you don't like the way it fits? Now's the time to get rid of it.

Consider whether a standard closet setup will work for you. With a pad and paper in hand, assess the amount of space your wardrobe currently occupies, from outerwear all the way to belts and jewelry. And don't assume that you need to double or triple your current space in order to make the project worthwhile—going way bigger than you actually need will let more time lapse between clean-outs, and the space can feel more confusing than a small, well-edited closet. Do you already have a large chest of drawers that has more than enough room for your sweaters? Then there's no need to plan closet space for sweaters. On the other hand, perhaps your purses have never had a logical place to go; a series of cubbies can help keep them in order. If, like most people, your wardrobe consists of separates, two rows of hanging bars, one over the other, may be a better use of space than just a single bar. Be sure to include enough hanging space for long skirts, coats, and gowns worn regularly. (Gowns that are worn very infrequently are best stored folded, rather than hung, as their weight can pull them out of shape over a period of time. Shake them out and refold on a yearly basis to avoid permanent creases.)

Include storage for accessories. Smaller cubbies can accommodate coiled belts, but if you have just a few belts, then several hooks along a wall can suffice. Shoe cubbies will help keep all your pairs organized and at the ready.

Since you've invested so much time and energy into your closet, don't stop short at hangers. Now is the time to invest in uniform, matching, wooden or fabric-padded hangers. Though they may seem extravagant, these hangers maintain even spacing in the closet, protect your clothing from pulling out of shape, and prevent that frustrating tangle that can happen with a mix of wire and plastic—and they'll go a long way to making your closet feel organized and neat.

CHAPTER FIVE hardworking spaces:

OFFICES, ENTRYWAYS, MUD-ROOMS, AND LAUNDRY ROOMS

compared with a newly streamlined kitchen, organizing your entryway, mudroom, laundry room, or office can seem rather dull. But it's not enough to arrange your kitchen, living room, bedroom, and bath and just hope that everything else falls into place. Without a plan, all too often the crannies of the home are forgotten, both decoratively and otherwise, and thus they become unruly quite quickly. These spaces arrive at this sorry state because we often ask more of them than we do of larger rooms. These are the places where we leave our coats and shoes, where we store spillover from other parts of the house, and where potentially messy chores are accomplished. These are transitional spaces that we burden with double and sometimes triple duty: the office that doubles as a craft center, the hallway connecting the bedrooms that has become home to textbooks and backpacks, and the entrance to a home—the classic parking place for everything

In the laundry room, where a good dose of cheer goes a long way, an antique dollhouse mounted on the wall with ornate wooden brackets functions as storage for supplies. Standing in for a plain laundry basket is a doll crib for folded linens, and a table topped with a towel provides a surface for spot cleaning and quick pressing.

that comes in the door. Disorder here can creep quickly into the serenity of the other rooms. Luckily, even small additions made here pay big dividends: A few hooks and a table by the front door can be enough to corral all jackets, bags, and shoes; a case of bookshelves in the hallway adds layers of richness and an additional place for books and artwork. Trunks, chests of drawers, and even armoires might sound like surprising additions to the hallway, but they can truly enhance the look of this space, providing a visual anchor and sense of scale—and of course, lots of storage space.

LEFT: An elegant collection of oars is both safely stored and beautifully displayed in this ingenious rack. Notches in the ledge across the bottom and in the bar across the middle hold each oar in place. Perfectly showcased, their natural hues and graceful shapes accent the rustic atmosphere created by the tree trunk and the camp chair.

RIGHT: Active families need a place to drop off coats, sweaters, boots, sports equipment, and countless other types of gear. Hooks, a table, and a bench or chair are imperative in a mudroom like this one, which handles a lot of traffic on a daily basis. The whimsical horseshoe hooks (made by affixing two horseshoes together at right angles) manage their job with style and invite good luck as well. A farmhouse table acts as a temporary repository for items waiting to be transported elsewhere, such as these terra-cotta pots and gardening tools. The diminutive pony can be put to use as a place to sit while removing muddy shoes or boots.

BELOW: An unexpected setup in the creamy white hallway of this weekend house is a first invitation upon entering to shake off the conventions of the everyday. Vintage medicine cabinets provide storage for each family member's weekend necessities, as well as a place to distribute mail or leave notes. White dining chairs underneath are spots to toss jackets or overnight bags, as well as a place to sit while lacing up shoes. Wall-mounted chairs add visual character.

ABOVE: In an addition to a historic eighteenth-century home, new owners made sure that the built-in closets suited the lines and materials of the original structure. In keeping with the Colonial style, the closet doors are paneled and fitted with handsome black iron hardware. The doors follow the slope of the roof in the rear of the house.

ABOVE: In an entryway already hinting at its owner's sense of fun—note the apple-green walls—a fire-engine-red can is useful as a repository for umbrellas and walking sticks as well as stylish. Built-in closets contribute to the clean lines of the cheerful entrance—one under the stairs can take boots or firewood, and a larger one next to the stairs holds coats.

ABOVE: Set underneath a staircase, no space is taken for granted in this office that Alice-in-Wonderland might keep. Bookshelves are cut to the angle of the overhead steps, and cubbies are installed underneath the desk. Drawers set right into the two bottom stairs will make fetching a pen or pencil a task that puts a smile on your face. Though the doors can be closed and the chair turned around to face the room when not in use, this setup is so appealing that you won't mind leaving it in view.

home-office storage

whether your desk fits into the cubby of an armoire or spreads several feet across a roomy home office, keeping desk supplies in order can be a challenge. To make the most of this work space, analyze your options: Are there enough shelves and drawers to accommodate files and office supplies, or do you need to supplement these with additional organizers? Start with the desktop, and work your way from there.

Think of the desktop like a kitchen countertop: Only keep out things that you use all the time, and if you work with paper files often, get a desktop vertical file holder for those you're currently working on. If not, there's no reason files should be on your desk.

Go vertical to save space: Secure a bulletin board above your desk to hang a calendar and important notices on, such as invitations, convention announcements, and reminders.

Create a spot for "action" papers. These are papers that need to be acted upon promptly, such as letters that require a quick response, bills, and so forth. This goes for non-paper items as well: If you have particular tools that you're currently working with, create a spot on or in your desk where they can all be stored for neatness' sake, but also so you can always find them.

Put financial files into long-term storage on a yearly basis, but keep one permanent file handy with things that you always want to be able to locate quickly, such as marriage and birth certificates, ownership papers for property and cars, passports, and other documents. For extra protection, consider storing them in fire-safe lockbox; or at least keep copies of everything somewhere other than your home, like a safe-deposit box.

Create a master list of the documents that you have stored in a special place so that you don't forget what's filed where. (Everyone thinks he'll remember, but he never does.) Make a list of these things, and keep a copy on your computer and a hard copy elsewhere, such as taped to the inside of a kitchen cabinet.

No office is complete without a wastebasket, which helps keep order by allowing you to toss what you don't need right away.

Customize storage to your office needs: Special magazine holders will keep magazines, catalogs, and brochures neat and orderly, and bookends will hold reference books in place.

A dining table tucked into an alcove makes a desk large enough to accommodate two. The bookcase mounted above lends it loads of useful space, and the cubbies of varied sizes create visual interest as well. Smaller ones along the bottom are fitted with baskets that function as pull-out trays. Hung in front of the bookcase is a favorite painting, which helps integrate the setup into the style of the rest of the room and provides a lovely place to rest your eyes when working at the desk.

OPPOSITE: A covered porch is the border between the house and the outdoors, and thus, both garden and indoor furniture fit in beautifully here. A great flea-market find, the iron cage houses a collection of watering cans and garden-theme items, such as urns and birdhouses. The bench and several decorative wall hangings complete the look.

ABOVE: Putting the results of a lifetime of collecting on display can create a unique, deeply personal effect that could never be achieved with wallpaper and decorator's tricks. This custom-built storage for model boats makes what would otherwise be a generic space into the defining décor of the upstairs. The rest of the hall is kept neutral with white paint and natural wood; little swaths of nautical hues from the boats themselves are all the color the space needs.

5 great ideas from this office

1 The vintage wire locker baskets hold individual projects that are in progress.

2 A curtain rod with café curtain clips provide gallery-like space to hang photos, postcards, or inspirational ephemera.

3 A bath towel bar was installed to hold the bright spools of ribbon. They add a splash of vibrant color to the work space in addition to being easy to access.

4 Cubbies, drawers, vintage cookie tins, baskets, and wire racks are just a few of the receptacles here that keep small items handy and add personality.

5 A thrift-shop desk was fitted with a painted plywood top that's longer than the desk. Flat shelves were installed under the additional length, creating more storage space underneath.

ABOVE: A seed packet display box from an old-fashioned garden store makes a logical desk accessory for anyone planning a garden, but it has charm enough for just sorting stationery as well. Though the desk itself only has one shallow drawer, the garden shelving has plenty of room to stash all your office supplies.

LEFT: Rows of modern, bracketless shelving around the upper perimeter of this potting room turn vases into an artful display. The rest of the room is similarly fitted for the gardener: Large cubbies under the counter hold urns and baskets for gathering cuttings, and a wide, deep sink is roomy enough for working on arrangements.

OPPOSITE: Porches are an extension of the house, especially during the summer. In order to make the porch a truly welcoming spot, you need to keep it just as clutter free as the rest of the house. Here, an undermounted storage trundle can hold magazines and toys, and is easily tucked away when guests arrive.

ABOVE: Every car should be equipped with an emergency kit; antique tin picnic baskets happen to be the perfect size for all the essentials, and you can tuck them away in a back corner of your trunk. Be sure to include jumper cables and roadside flares, a pressure gauge for tires, first-aid supplies, a flashlight, a road map of your most-traveled locations, and a few bottles of water and granola bars.

LEFT: A series of notches cut into shelves is a clever solution for storing galoshes and keeping the floor clear. Hanging them upside down allows them to dry completely, without dripping into the boots hung beneath.

ABOVE: In a casual entrance with a closet, consider a curtain instead of a closet door. Raincoats and muddy boots can be concealed in an instant, freeing a peg rail and a shelf, with elegant curved brackets, for garden supplies.

LABEL IT In your enthusiasm to stow away boxes and bins filled with items to be stored for a long time, don't forget to label the containers. When it comes time to find something, you'll want to locate the correct container at a glance.

ABOVE & RIGHT: Hardworking storage is the key to a well-organized garage. Draw on shelves, cubbies, cabinets, and bins to corral the tools, sports equipment, car parts, and toys that tend to accumulate in this space. Label each box or bin so one glance will help you find what you are after. A wall of Peg Board keeps screwdrivers, clamps, and other tools accessible and in view. Keeping the space white imparts a crisp, clean feeling while the red accents prevent it from looking sterile. A basket rounds up a collection of balls. There's a place for everything here, including room to tuck a small refrigerator under the worktable.

sorting through long-term storage

when it comes to the basement, garage, and attic, aesthetic considerations rarely come into play—we'd rather focus our efforts on the visible rooms of the house. But ignoring these spaces can make navigating them more difficult than necessary. Here are tips for keeping these areas usable:

- Attics are prone to intense heat, and basements to moisture. Store treasured photographs and collectibles vulnerable to the elements in bedroom or main-floor closets rather than one of these two spaces.

- Whenever you pass through the basement or attic, give all your storage a quick once-over to make sure that everything is in good condition and hasn't become damp or gnawed by pests.

- The basement is particularly prone to becoming a dumping ground for the whole family; weed things out every six months.

- In the attic, do not store anything in plastic bags, which can melt in extreme heat, trap moisture, and promote mold and mildew. Instead, look for tightly woven cotton garment bags for clothing and acid-free boxes for other keepsakes.

- Create an inventory, label and number the boxes, and keep a list of their contents in a safe place.

- In the basement, invest in a dehumidifier and keep everything off the floor on risers or shelves to protect boxes and items from water in case of flood.

- When storing anything valuable in the attic, be sure to drape it loosely with a plastic dropcloth to protect it from leaks overhead.

A former storage cabinet for nuts and bolts from a hardware store anchors the décor of this hallway, bringing a touch of informality to the casually elegant space. And since it's in the hallway, it can pick up the storage slack from any of the surrounding rooms, like sewing supplies, extra lightbulbs, and miscellaneous household tools.

ABOVE: Easy accessibility maximizes efficiency. Long, open shelves keep laundry necessities within easy reach. Clear jars let you see exactly how much detergent you have left. And a peg rail can hold hand towels, hangers—even a watering can—at the ready.

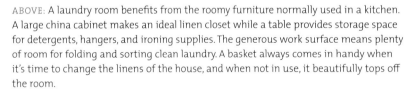

ABOVE: A laundry room benefits from the roomy furniture normally used in a kitchen. A large china cabinet makes an ideal linen closet while a table provides storage space for detergents, hangers, and ironing supplies. The generous work surface means plenty of room for folding and sorting clean laundry. A basket always comes in handy when it's time to change the linens of the house, and when not in use, it beautifully tops off the room.

OPPOSITE: Just because it happens to be the site of chores doesn't mean the laundry room has to look dull. A wall of shelves painted apple green (and complemented with feminine floral wallpaper) functions as an extension of the linen closet. A collection of baskets makes the sorting and transport of laundry easy, but when not in use, they convert the shelves into a makeshift chest of drawers; even when full, they're light enough to easily pull out and lift.

OPPOSITE: At one end of an open-plan living and dining room, a full wall of built-in shelves and drawers creates a charming nook of a home office. It can be a challenge to combine an office with a public room of the house, but it works here due to beautiful shelving—which complements the décor of the rest of the room—and the fact that there's plenty of decorative display mixed with the practical. Shelves, drawers, and pullout baskets help sort business and pleasure, and a bulletin board backing in the main desk cubby carves out a spot to pin up notes.

RIGHT: A renovation to a farmhouse allowed the homeowners to custom design a mudroom. The wide Shaker-style hutch stores and displays collectibles, including Pennsylvania stoneware crocks, nineteenth-century yellowware bowls, animal figures, and jugs. An early-twentieth-century pack basket, an attractive decoration, is also handy for picnics. The orange-painted American pine cupboard, which dates to the 1850s, keeps shoes tucked away when not in use.

BE INSPIRED Your home office should delight you and fill you with inspiration. Peruse books about artists' and writers' studios for ideas about decorating and organizing your work space.

OPPOSITE: In a room too tight for a regular desk, the spindly legs of a simple sawhorse table maintain a light, airy feel. A tiny wooden box affixed to the back of the wooden chair acts as desk drawer of sorts, holding notebooks and pens. The bookshelves, filing cabinet, and wall colors contribute a sense of playfulness—perfect for inspiring creativity while working.

RIGHT: Many vintage armoires are tall and deep. Fitted with a shelf for a computer and a pullout drawer for a keyboard, this space makes a compact office that can be folded away—a particularly good feature in a boy's room, where spontaneous chaos can occasionally erupt. Here, a bulletin board is mounted on the inside of the door, and drawers provide storage for school supplies.

OPPOSITE: In many homes, the laundry room is an afterthought, considered a mere utility room. But to make the most of your laundry room, organization is key. Here, an alcove has been fitted with shelves and dedicated to storing clean laundry. Individual baskets make it easy to sort the clothes and linens, and each basket is labeled with a name tag so that family members can quickly identify which one is theirs. Simple curtains of ticking fabric hung on a rod conceal under-sink storage with a casual, countrified look. Stash a laundry basket, trash can, or spare bottles or boxes of laundry detergent underneath, but be mindful of children or pets. Above the washer and dryer is a wide countertop that's perfect for folding laundry. You may want to install a small television or radio to help pass the time while folding and ironing. A peg rail is perfect for hanging delicates or damp items to dry.

SHAKER STYLE Peg rails are a Shaker tradition and can be cut to fit a wall space of any size—short or long—and installed in any room of the house.

ABOVE: Winter boots and coats—that's the kind of stuff you want to hide away. But when it's sun hats and sandals at a beach cottage, catching sight of them just reinforces a sense of breezy relaxation. Here, a peg rail is a place to hang hats and beach bags; baskets fitted to their shelves can hold towels, sun block, extra flip-flops, and whatever else might be carried in and out of the house.

Photography Credits

Page 1: Steven Randazzo
Page 2: Keith Scott Morton
Page 6: Robin Stubbert
Page 8: Andrew McCaul
Page 12: Keith Scott Morton
Pages 14–15: Dominique Vorillon
Page 16: Keith Scott Morton
Page 17: Michael Luppino
Page 18 (top): Steven Randazzo
Page 18 (bottom): Keith Scott Morton
Page 19: Keith Scott Morton
Pages 20–21: Keith Scott Morton
Page 21 (top): Keith Scott Morton
Page 21 (bottom): Keith Scott Morton
Page 22: Steven Randazzo
Page 24: Julian Wass
Page 25: William P. Steele
Page 26: Keith Scott Morton
Page 27: Gridley & Graves
Page 28: Michael Luppino
Page 29: Michael Luppino
Pages 30–31: Michael Luppino
Page 32: Steven Randazzo
Page 33: Michael Luppino
Page 34 (left): Gridley & Graves
Page 34 (right): Laura Resen
Page 35: Michael Luppino
Page 37: Keith Scott Morton
Page 38: Gridley & Graves
Page 39 (left): Steven Randazzo
Page 39 (right): Keith Scott Morton
Page 40: Keith Scott Morton
Pages 42–43: Keith Scott Morton
Page 44: Steven Randazzo
Page 45: Steven Randazzo
Pages 46–47: Jonn Coolidge
Page 47: Jonn Coolidge
Page 48: Michael Luppino

Page 49 (left): Andrew McCaul
Page 49 (right): Andrew McCaul
Pages 50–51: Grey Crawford
Page 51: Keith Scott Morton
Pages 52–53 (all): Keith Scott Morton
Pages 54–55 (all): Michael Luppino
Pages 56–57: Jeff McNamara
Page 58 (top): Laura Resen
Page 58 (bottom): Pierre Chanteau
Page 59: Jonn Coolidge
Pages 60–61: Keith Scott Morton
Page 61: Keith Scott Morton
Page 62: Keith Scott Morton
Page 63 (all): William P. Steele
Page 64: Keith Scott Morton
Page 66: Keith Scott Morton
Pages 66–67: Keith Scott Morton
Page 68: Keith Scott Morton
Page 69: Keith Scott Morton
Page 70 (top): Steven Randazzo
Page 70 (bottom): Keith Scott Morton
Page 71: Keith Scott Morton
Page 72: William P. Steele
Page 73 (left): William P. Steele
Page 73 (right): William P. Steele
Pages 74–75: William P. Steele
Page 76: Keith Scott Morton
Page 77: Dominique Vorillon
Page 78 (left): Keith Scott Morton
Page 78 (right): Keith Scott Morton
Page 79 (left): Gridley & Graves
Page 79 (right): Keith Scott Morton
Page 80 (top left): Keith Scott Morton
Page 80 (top middle): Robin Stubbert
Page 80 (top right): Michael Luppino

Page 80 (bottom): Michael Luppino
Page 81: Michael Luppino
Page 82 (left): Keith Scott Morton
Page 82 (right): Keith Scott Morton
Page 83 (left): Keith Scott Morton
Page 83 (right): Robin Stubbert
Page 84: Stacey Brandford
Page 86 (left): Gridley & Graves
Page 86 (right): Keith Scott Morton
Page 87 (all): William P. Steele
Page 88 (top): Keith Scott Morton
Page 88 (bottom): Keith Scott Morton
Page 89 (left): Keith Scott Morton
Page 89 (right): Keith Scott Morton
Page 90: Keith Scott Morton
Page 92 (left): Keith Scott Morton
Page 92 (right): Keith Scott Morton
Page 93: Keith Scott Morton
Page 94: Keith Scott Morton
Page 95: Keith Scott Morton
Pages 96–97: Keith Scott Morton
Page 98: Keith Scott Morton
Page 99: Keith Scott Morton
Page 100: Gridley & Graves
Page 102 (left): Keith Scott Morton
Page 102 (right): Keith Scott Morton
Page 103: Keith Scott Morton
Page 104 (left): Keith Scott Morton
Page 104 (right): Keith Scott Morton
Page 105 (left): Laura Resen
Page 105 (right): Stacey Brandford
Page 106: Michael Luppino
Page 107 (left): Grey Crawford
Page 107 (right): Keith Scott Morton
Page 108: Andrew McCaul and Catherine Gratwicke
Page 110: Keith Scott Morton
Page 111: Keith Scott Morton
Page 112 (left): Keith Scott Morton

Page 112 (right): Keith Scott Morton
Page 113: Keith Scott Morton
Page 114: Stacey Brandford
Page 116: Steven Randazzo
Pages 116–117: Keith Scott Morton
Page 118 (left): Keith Scott Morton
Page 118 (right): Laura Resen
Page 119 (left): Keith Scott Morton
Page 119 (right): Keith Scott Morton
Page 120: Robin Stubbert
Page 121 (left): Robin Stubbert
Page 121 (right): Robin Stubbert
Page 122: Steven Randazzo
Page 124 (all): Lucas Allen
Page 125 (left): Keith Scott Morton
Page 125 (right): Keith Scott Morton
Page 126: Pascal Blancon

Page 127 (left): Grey Crawford
Page 127 (right): Keith Scott Morton
Page 128 (left): Keith Scott Morton
Page 128 (right): Keith Scott Morton
Page 130: Keith Scott Morton
Page 132: Keith Scott Morton
Pages 132–133: Chuck Baker
Page 134 (left): Keith Scott Morton
Page 134 (right): Keith Scott Morton
Page 135 (left): Gridley & Graves
Page 135: Jonn Coolidge
Page 136: Keith Scott Morton
Page 138: Grey Crawford
Page 139: Jessie Walker
Pages 140–141: Steven Randazzo
Page 141: Keith Scott Morton
Page 142: Jeff McNamara

Page 143: Michael Luppino
Page 144 (top left): Andrew McCaul
Page 144 (bottom left): Tim Street-Porter
Page 144 (right): Gridley & Graves
Page 145 (left): Keith Scott Morton
Page 145 (right): Keith Scott Morton
Page 146: Steven Randazzo
Page 148 (left): Natasha Milne
Page 148 (right): Keith Scott Morton
Page 149: Keller + Keller
Page 150: William P. Steele
Page 151: Gridley & Graves
Page 152: David Prince
Page 153: Keith Scott Morton
Page 154 (all): Keith Scott Morton
Page 155: Keith Scott Morton

Index